INCREDIBLE INSECTS!

Eye-opening Photos of Amazing Bugs

playBac
PUBLISHING
More.Brain.Power

Insects are amazing! There are more types of insects on earth than any other living creature!

In fact, 95% of all animal species are insects! They are very important to the breakdown of all sorts of plant and animal matter, and they are a major food source for many other animal species.

Taken by photographers who are passionate about creepy crawly things, these photos capture bugs in a whole new way. In the following pages, you will see delicate wings, stinky things, hard workers, and camouflage lurkers, beautiful, hairy, and plenty of scary bugs! You'll learn fascinating facts about wasps, mantises, butterflies, crickets, caterpillars, katydids, toktokkies . . . and many, many more!

Turn the page to begin your journey on a bugs-eye-view of the insect world.

Weevils are also known as "snout beetles." Can you guess why? The most defining physical characteristic of the weevil is its long nose (or snout), which it uses to chew its way deep into plants. This process provides two results for the weevil: a tasty vegetarian dinner as well as a protective hole in which to lay its eggs. Because both the chewing and the egg laying can destroy a plant, weevils are considered to be some of the most serious insect pests in the United States. Weevils damage fruit and cotton crops as well as dry foods like cereals, grains, nuts, and seeds. They are members of the beetle family with the distinction of having noses that are longer than their bodies!

A dragonfly of habit.

Called "skimmers" because they fly low over the water, the black-tailed skimmer dragonfly often follows the same path and returns to rest on a familiar perch. They stay close to the water in search of their favorite meals: mosquitoes, midges, winged ants, and flies. Each skimmer has two pairs of large, delicate wings, which extend out from its body when it is at rest. Whether hiding in the tall grass or flying over the open water, skimmers know how to navigate!

"Is this thing on?"

Despite its name, the lantern bug does not glow or emit light! They are named after the bright, contrasting colors on their wings and nose, which is also called a rostrum. Found primarily in the tropics, these bugs use their specialized rostrums to suck juice out of flowers and fruit, but not to find their way in the dark!

This feeding frenzy is a blur of blue!

One-fifth of the 1.5 million different insect species living on planet earth are beetles! That would explain the rush for lunch! These Mexican blue beetles are all trying to get a piece of the same leafy stalk but, in reality, beetles can eat almost anything: plants, other insects, rotting carcasses, and even manure. Maybe that's why they have survived for so long and in such great numbers; researchers now believe that beetles have been around for over 200 million years!

"I'm outstanding in my field!"

Grasshoppers can be found almost everywhere in the world, except for the colder regions near the North and South poles. In fact, there are over 10,000 species of grasshoppers! They live in fields, meadows, and just about anywhere they can find generous amounts of leaves to eat. This rain forest grasshopper is one of the more uncommon-looking varieties of a very common insect!

"I couldn't eat a thing!"

Midges hatch from eggs that are laid on the surface of water in gelatinous masses that can contain up to 3,000 eggs each. Because they occur in such huge numbers, and because they spend their entire early life (as pale pink larvae) in the water, midges are an important food source for fish. But don't worry about a huge population of hungry midges invading anytime soon: The dark red adults live for only three to five days and, during that time, they *never* eat!

13

small, but tricky.

Most ladybugs are less than a quarter inch long. Their small size makes them attractive to predators looking for a tasty treat, but ladybugs can be quite tricky. Their red-and-black color sends a message of "danger" to other insects. And if threatened, a ladybug will pull up her legs and play dead, turtle-style. Ladybugs live in a wide variety of habitats including trees, fields, lawns, and beaches, and they are very good at playing it safe!

You are what you eat.

The beautiful blue morpho butterfly is one of the most recognizable in the world. These iridescent butterflies live in tropical forests, seeking out sunny clearings in which to warm themselves. They are unsteady flyers, wobbling as they move through the air, so they are easily caught. But predators beware! Adult blue morphos are poisonous, due to the foods they consume while still in the caterpillar stage.

standing guard for the queen.

Yellow jacket wasps can be easily identified by their distinctive markings of alternating bands of bright yellow. They build their nests in the ground, in hollow logs, or attached to branches and buildings, by chewing wood fiber into a paperlike pulp. Their homes are their castles, and worker yellow jackets—who are about half an inch long—are very protective about their queen. They don't "sting and run" but are known to use their lance-like stingers repeatedly. Ouch!

Beware the assassin!

These wheel bugs are part of the assassin bug family, and their family name is well deserved. Using a needlelike beak, these bugs immobilize their prey within 30 seconds of capture by injecting their deadly saliva into any soft spot they can find. The toxic saliva contains a paralyzing substance that allows the wheel bug to quickly suck out all the victim's bodily fluids. What appears to be a long antenna actually functions more like a straw: slurp!

These beetles simply don't waste the waste!

Dung beetles are capable of rolling balls of dung that are up to 50 times their own weight! But what are they doing with all that poop? They suck liquid from the manure, which serves as their main meal. (Gross, but true!) They roll it into tennis ball–size spheres, which they bury, then crawl under to mate. And, finally, the female dung beetle lays her eggs inside the balls of manure to protect her young beetle family. The dung beetles' handy use and reuse of all that manure is helpful to farmers, livestock, and their own well-being.

Not just another pretty butterfly.

The beautiful clearwing butterfly—also known as the "glasswing"—can be identified by the brown edges, white bars, and completely clear areas on each of its wings. The large, clear patches help camouflage the clearwings while they fly from flower to flower, feeding on nectar. Their transparent wings make them tricky to spot and very difficult for predators to identify. They are pretty, and pretty clever!

We're shy, but we like to play ball!

Pill bugs, also known as "sow bugs" or "roly-polies," like to be inconspicuous and stay out of sight. They live in damp places under stones and logs, feeding on moss, algae, bark, and other decaying matter. They remain hidden during the day and become active only at night. When these tiny bugs are uncovered, they roll up into a tight ball—the favorite defense mechanism of shy roly-polies.

"I don't want to live in a jewelry box!"

Many beetles, such as this silver scarab beetle, have shiny metallic shells. They are hard to miss, and are particularly attractive to collectors. The ancient Egyptians revered scarab beetles. They created a special "beetle" hieroglyph, incorporated them into tombs, and offered them as ceremonial gifts. The image of the beetle was often recreated as jewelry, but some cultures have gone so far as to string together necklaces from the real thing!

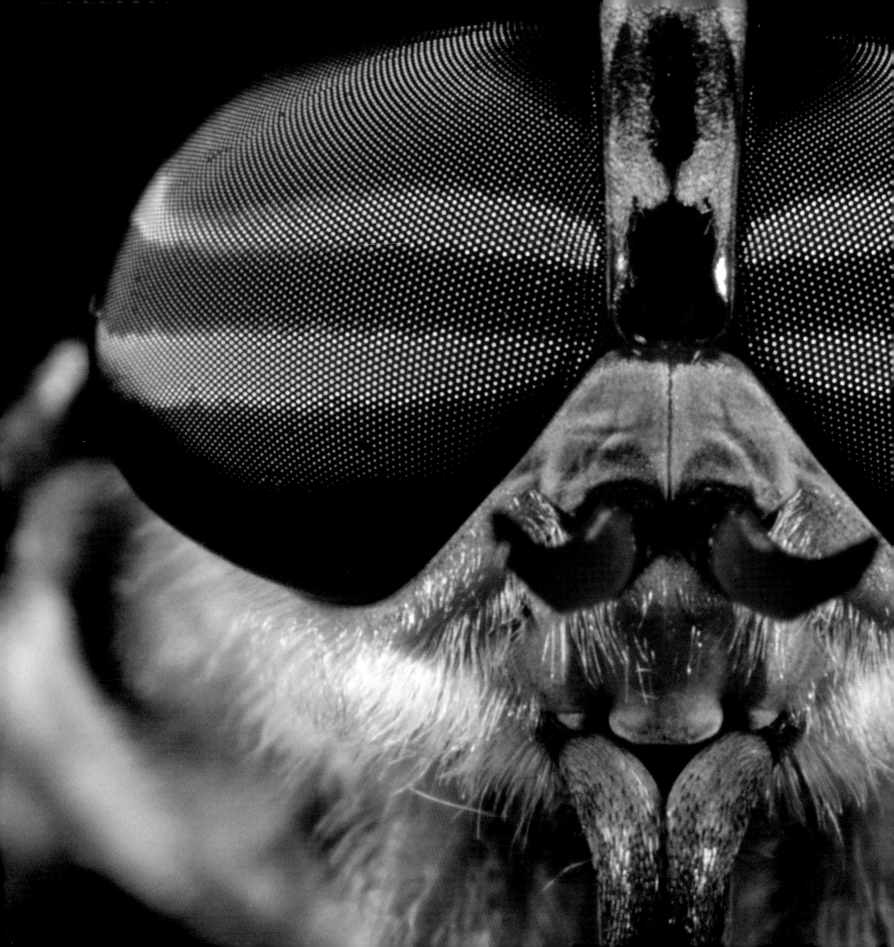

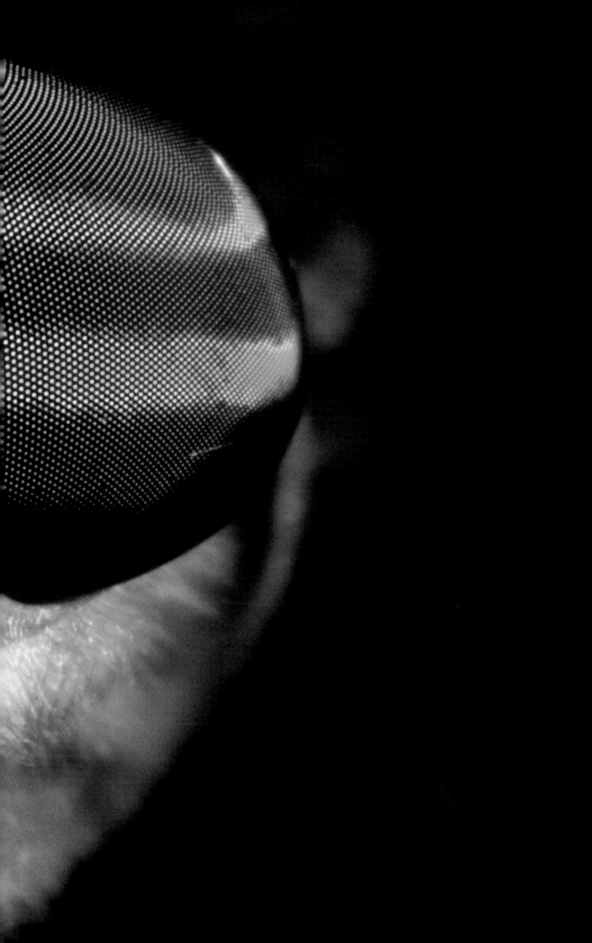

what are you looking at?

Horseflies have solid-colored bodies, clear wings, and brightly colored eyes. Each horsefly eye contains up to 30,000 lenses! All the better to see you with, my dear! They are very common bloodsucking insects that prey on cattle, horses, and even humans. And you can bet they have no problem locating dinner!

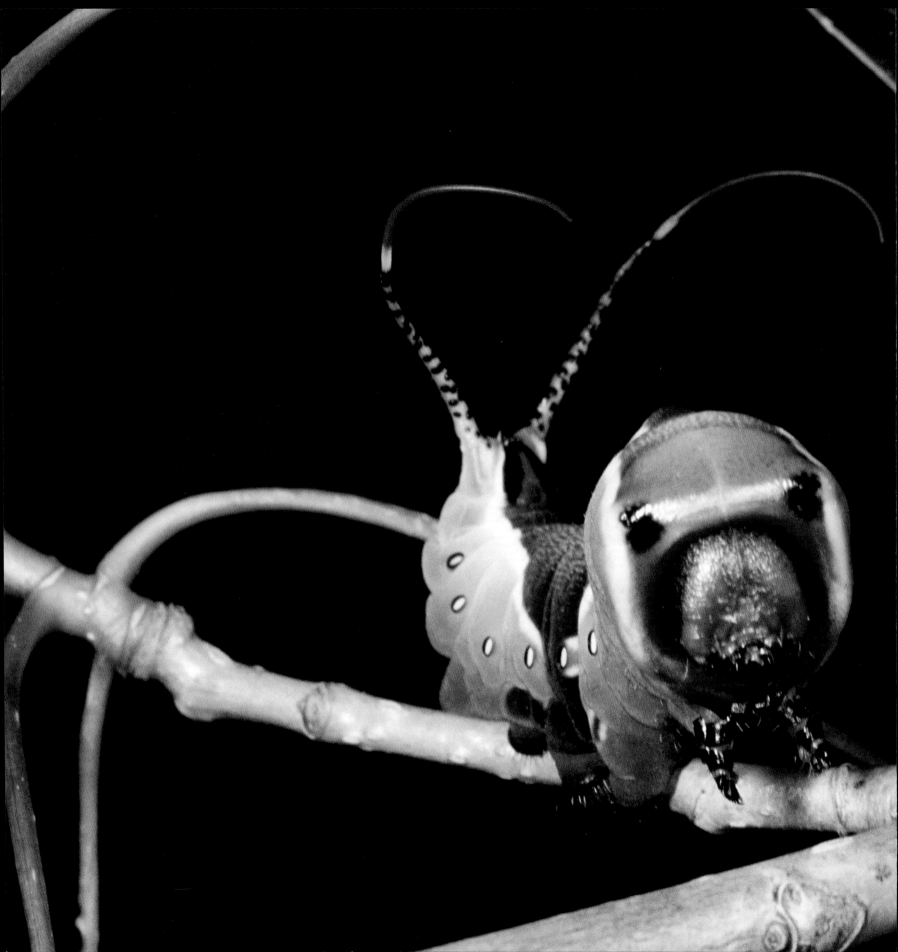

"Fooled you! That's not my face!"

Caterpillars, like this puss moth variety, feed on the leaves of many shrubs and bushes. In order to eat in peace and avoid predators, they develop backsides that resemble front sides! These "false faces" give the appearance of an alert, watchful caterpillar so that the caterpillar's actual face can search for food undisturbed. Confused predators can never be sure if the puss moth caterpillar is coming or going!

Got milkweed?

Milkweed bugs are sometimes found by the hundreds on a single plant. They are one of a very small group of insects that can eat the seeds and tolerate the poisonous compounds found in the sap of the milkweed plant. Birds learn to stay away from the orange-and-black bugs, who taste as toxic as they look. As you can imagine, milkweed bugs have very few predators!

I'm not as innocent as I look!

May beetles—also known as "June bugs"—can cause considerable plant damage. The adults are defoliators, meaning that they chew the leaves of trees and shrubs. They are nocturnal, preferring to feed (and do their damage) at night. The young May beetle grubs live in the soil and feed on the roots of plants. When present in great numbers, these innocent-looking bugs can be very destructive!

Ready for take-off.

Short-horned grasshoppers do not have actual horns. It is their stout antenna that gives them their name. Most species live in grasslands, where they feast on a variety of leaves and grasses, and even the occasional weak or dead grasshopper. Like their locust cousins, short-horned grasshoppers sometimes form very large swarms that coordinate migrations and can be highly destructive to plant life.

Please keep your saliva to yourself.

Adult mosquitoes feed on nectar and plant juices, but only the female feeds on blood, too. She needs blood to help in the development of eggs, and she gets it from birds, reptiles, and mammals—including humans. During feeding, mosquitoes inject saliva into the bodies of their "hosts" as they draw blood out, making female mosquitoes carriers and transmitters of major diseases such as malaria and yellow fever. Mosquito bites become very itchy for humans because we are actually allergic to their saliva!

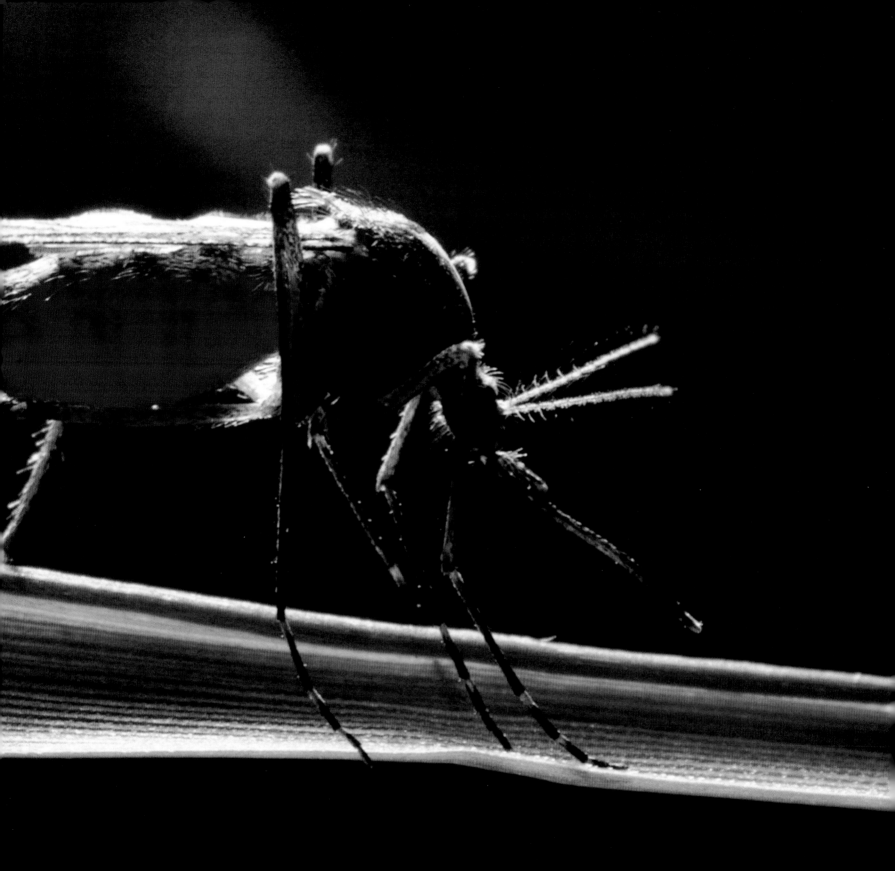

Eat or be eaten!

Yellow mealworms are the larvae form of the mealworm beetle. They are well-known for infesting stored food products such as flour, grain, and cereal. They like dark hiding places and can be very hard to get rid of once they've made themselves at home in your pantry. But when they aren't eating someone out of house and home, mealworms themselves—also known as "golden grubs"—make excellent food for aquarium fish and animals in zoos.

whoa! Steady there, Pardner!

Longhorn beetles are characterized by their extremely long antennae, which are often longer than the beetle's body! This golden-bloomed grey longhorn seems to be trying to steady himself from tipping under the weight of his immense headgear. Although they feed on leaves, fruit, bark, sap, and fungi, the longhorns' main goal appears to be staying upright!

oil and Vinegaroon, anyone?

Because of their poor eyesight, vinegaroon bugs use their long, thin front legs like walking sticks to tap and feel their way around. Vinegaroons are often confused with scorpions. They aren't poisonous and they don't sting, but they sure can pinch. And they do carry a secret weapon: The vinegaroon is capable of spraying a vinegar-scented mist from its underside when disturbed. Great for attacking predators; not so great on salads.

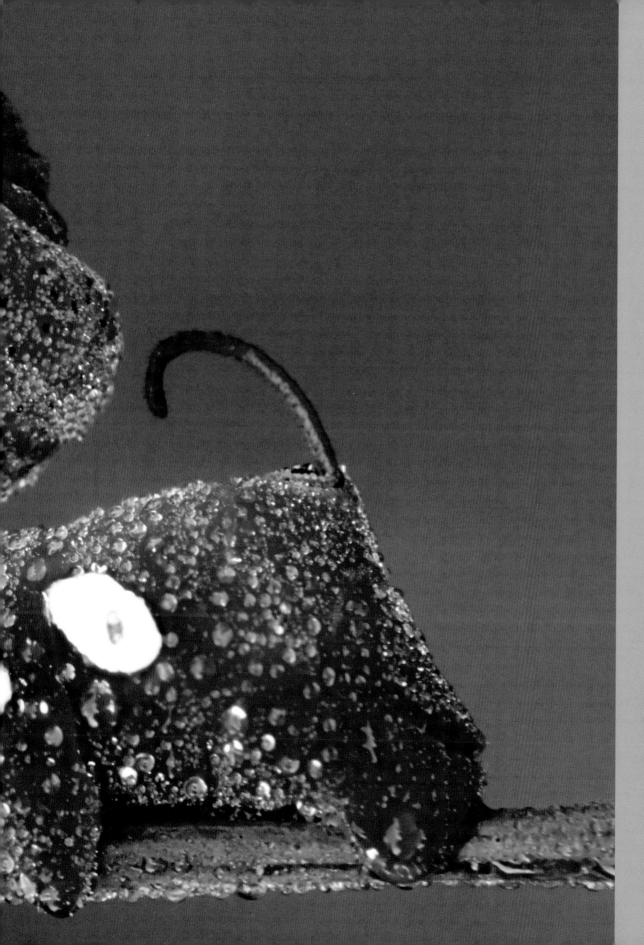

This sphinx has left the desert.

The stunning pandora sphinx moth caterpillar often holds its body upright in a sphinxlike position. It is this posture, along with the five oval white spots on its side, that defines the sphinx caterpillar's signature look. The "horn" on its tail end will eventually be replaced by a small buttonlike spot. The fashionable caterpillar shown here is in perfect partial camouflage to the red stem as it chews a leaf.

Don't call me "Fido"!

Flower beetles are members of the scarab family. This yellow-and-brown specimen would barely be noticed among the dead wood and leaf litter that are its food sources. Flower beetles are known for their brightly colored, prismatic shells— occasionally displaying a rainbow of dazzling colors. Some people are so attracted to the patterns and colors of these beetles, they actually keep them as pets!

I wouldn't giddyup if I were you!

The distinctive brown-on-green saddle of the saddleback moth caterpillar may look like an inviting mount, but: beware! Protective clusters of spines line the sides of the "saddle" as well as the front and back ends. These spines are capable of inflicting painful and lasting stings. What may look "furry and cute" is—in this case—quite nasty and harmful!

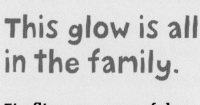

This glow is all in the family.

Fireflies are some of the most easily recognizable insects. Their light is the beautiful result of a complex set of scientific phenomena. While in flight, the males emit a flash every 5.5 seconds, sending an important signal to females on the ground. The females flash their responses 2 seconds later, disclosing their locations. Their lights, and their timing are crucial to the firefly mating ritual. Interestingly, firefly eggs also emit a slight glow, as do young firefly larvae, often referred to as "glowworms."